LEARNING TO SAY GOOD-BY

LEARNING TO SAY GOOD-BY

EDA LeSHAN

Illustrated by Paul Giovanopoulos

AVON
PUBLISHERS OF BARD, CAMELOT AND DISCUS BOOKS

Acknowledgments: I would like to express my gratitude to the following people who read this manuscript and offered their suggestions and criticisms: Anne Appelbaum, Sylvia Halpern, Edgar Jackson, Beverly Kennedy, Ann Kliman, Lawrence LeShan, Nan Litvak, Florence Miale, and David Reuther. A special word of thanks to children's librarian Dorothy Gunzenhauser for providing much of the bibliography.

This book is lovingly dedicated to the memory of
Bob Kennedy, host of "Kennedy and Co.,"
ABC-TV, Chicago, and to Elizabeth and Suzanne,
the lovely, wise, brave daughters he left
as a legacy to the world.

CONTENTS

LEARNING TO SAY GOOD-BY

INTRODUCTION

꒰◉(|)◉꒱

Dear Reader:

Some people may find this book shocking. There are those who believe that children should be "protected" from talk about death and dying, that painful experiences which are not discussed will just go away and be forgotten. This is wrong. We now know that this is just a temporary masking of feelings which can be very hurtful to us all through our lives. What I have learned from many years of working with children and their families and from my own experience is that the most important part of living through a terrible experience is to understand and accept your feelings.

Experts in understanding human emotions have

been working with people who are mourning for someone they love. What they have found is that the families who try to run away from their feelings suffer longer and often never recover from their grief. Families who face their loss and all the feelings that go with it, who learn to accept all the normal stages of grief human beings seem to need to go through, become stronger and are able to begin to go on growing and living full and satisfying lives.

That is why this book will deal very frankly with all the kinds of things we know happen to people when someone they love dies. There is no feeling or experience in this book that hasn't happened to perfectly normal parents and children.

I hope your family will read this book and talk about it with one another. At first talking it over may be too hard, and if it is, don't try. Sometimes it is comforting just to know that you are sharing similar thoughts and ideas, without discussing them. Later on you may feel like going back to some of what you read earlier and talking it over. Even if you disagree with some of the ideas in the book, it still may help to think it over.

Every person has a right to his or her private thoughts and feelings. Some parents and children will find that while they might find it helpful to read this book together, there are some parts of it that they would rather not share openly with each other. That's O.K., too. It is important to respect each other's feelings about that.

One of the reasons I wanted to write this book is because of something that happened to my mother when she was four years old. Her mother died. Nobody told her the truth about what had happened—they felt she was too young. She kept asking people where her mother was, and they told her that her mother was sick, and had gone to the country to rest.

My mother saw that all her relatives were suffering, but no one would tell her why. Because she was so young, and because nobody explained the facts, my mother decided that she must have been a very bad little girl and that her mother had left her because she didn't love her. For many months she suffered from terrible loneliness and fear and anger at herself and everyone else, including her mother whom she felt had deserted her. Then she heard some neighbors discussing her mother's death. She learned the truth from strangers, not from the people she loved and needed to trust.

This experience was so hurtful that my mother lived with painful memories all her life. She helped me to understand that a child can live through *anything,* so long as he or she is told the truth and is allowed to share with loved ones the natural feelings people have when they are suffering. You will be far better able to live through your grief if you do it together, holding on tight to each other and trusting each other.

Eda LeShan
New York, October 1975

IT HAS
HAPPENED

Just about the most terrible thing that can happen to a child is the death of a parent. Most children feel as if the world has come to an end, as if their own life is over. This is a normal and natural way to feel—but it is not the truth. The truth is that you will feel a terrible sadness for a long, long time. You will feel frightened and angry—but after many, many months, these feelings will become less painful and occur less often. You will find yourself picking up the threads of your life, even looking toward the future with hope and pleasure. Good things will happen once again.

Probably you can't think about the future right now. If your parent has died very recently, you may feel numb. You just can't believe it. You keep thinking, "This must be a nightmare I am having —oh please, please, let me wake up!"

This is the first stage of grief over the death of someone you love and need. We seem to feel this way whether or not we knew ahead of time that the person was going to die. Even when a parent is very sick for a long time and everyone seems very frightened and worried, death is almost as much of a shock as if it happened quite suddenly and un-expectedly. The reason for this is that the death of someone close to us is something for which we cannot prepare ourselves. When it happens it is always unbelievable.

Human beings are the only living creatures who know that someday they will die. Yet no matter how much we try to understand and accept the fact of death, it seems unbearable and impossible that this living person, this special person, this person who is like no one else in all the world, could die.

At first, disbelief may be the strongest feeling you have. This is nature's way of helping you through the first stage of grief—deadening the pain a little, giving you time to absorb the facts.

As the hours and days pass—or sometimes even weeks and months later—you begin to feel the truth. You long for the person who is missing. You ache to feel his or her arms around you. You would give anything—everything—for the sight of his or her face, the sound of his or her voice. As you begin to realize this will never happen, feelings of terror begin. Without this person you feel you just cannot go on living.

Soon you may begin to have angry feelings. "How could someone who really loved me leave me alone like this?" You might think, "What a terrible thing to do to a little child!" Then you will probably begin to feel guilty. Maybe, in some way, this was your fault. Did you make too much noise while Daddy was sick? Did Mom get sick because you and your brothers made her work too hard?

As the days pass it will help if you realize that these feelings happen to everyone, but that doesn't mean they are accurate. Human beings get a lot of confused, mixed-up ideas about things—especially when they are most upset. What we need to do as time goes on is to understand our feelings and accept them, and then begin to figure out which feelings really make sense to us and which ones do not.

THE WAY GROWNUPS BEHAVE

From the moment you found out that your mother or father had died, other people seemed to be telling you how to feel and what to do. Kathy and her brother Kenneth, aged eight and ten, were in school. Their mother was at the hospital with their father, who had been sick for three or four months. One day, they were called out of their classes and rushed into a neighbor's car. As they were driving to their house, the neighbor said, "I have very sad news to tell you. Your daddy has died. Your mother is on the way home from the hospital and asked me to pick you up. Now I know you are going to help her by being very brave and strong. Your daddy wouldn't want you to cry."

When they got to their house, Aunt Jean was waiting for them. She was crying. She held out her arms to them and hugged them tight. She said, "That's right, my darlings, cry as much as you need to. This is a terrible, terrible thing that has happened. I love you so much. Your daddy loved you so much, and you loved him. We need to cry together."

Grownups usually behave in ways they were taught by their own parents when they were young. They want to be helpful and to do what they believe is right. But sometimes they are wrong. The neighbor was mistaken. It is both natural and necessary to let real feelings happen. It is not a sign of being weak or cowardly. When a terrible hurt is felt we need to cry. We need to be held and to hold each other; we need to feel love around us.

When I was a little girl, I saw something happen

that taught me a lot about mourning for someone you love. It was summer, and the father of the two little boys next door died very suddenly. Their mother's sorrow was so great that she didn't want her sons to see how much she was suffering. Jerry and Lee were taken care of by their aunt while their mother went away for several weeks. Some days they came out to play as if nothing had happened. Other days they were very quiet and wanted to be left alone. I never saw either one of them cry. When their mother came back, she got out of the car and ran over to them with her arms outstretched. Quick as a flash, Jerry and Lee ran away—down the road and off into some nearby woods. Their mother was shocked and hurt. When they didn't come back, she became very worried. It took the police and many of the neighbors several hours to find the children and bring them home. I can remember feeling that I understood why the boys had run away from their mother. She had run away from them when they needed her the most. They were angry at her and felt she was like a stranger.

Some grownups are so upset themselves that they cannot bear to see a child suffering. They think the best thing to do is to try to protect a child from seeing how they really feel. Ellen's grandfather died when she was eight years old, and her parents did not let her go to the funeral. They felt it would be too upsetting for Ellen to see so many people crying. She was left at home with a baby-sitter. When her family came home after the funeral, they told her to go and play in her own room while all the relatives and friends sat in the living room. Ellen had loved her grandfather very much and she felt awful. She stood at her bedroom window looking out, wondering what you do to live through so much sadness, but she didn't know what to do. She felt so lonely, so shut out from the people she loved and needed. She wanted to cry, she wanted her family to hug her and hold her tight. Being all alone made her feel too frightened to cry.

Many years later, when Ellen was a grown woman, her own mother died. She took her little boy, who was only five years old, to the funeral. Some of her relatives thought she was doing a cruel and foolish thing. But she remembered how she had felt when her grandfather had died and she did not want the same thing to happen to David.

When they got to the cemetery, she began to cry. David was very upset at seeing his mother so unhappy. Ellen bent over, picked him up, and hugged him. She said, "Yes, David, I feel so sad. It's hard for me to say good-by to Grandma. But holding you and loving you is a great help. When someone we love dies we need to be with people we love. I know you miss Grandma too, and I want to hold you when you feel like crying."

David began to cry. Ellen's aunt said, "See what

you've done? Look how upset he is. How could you do that to such a young child?" Ellen knew that she was helping David by showing him that there are some things worth crying about, and that holding tight to each other was the most important comfort for both of them. David would not feel alone and shut out as she had once felt.

PLANNING FOR THE FUNERAL

Grownups have different ideas about whether or not children should be allowed to go to the funeral home, to see the body in the coffin, to go to the funeral services and the cemetery.

Generally, it is up to the parent who is still alive to decide on the kind of burial. If a parent is not sure what he or she wants to do and the children are old enough to know what is going on and to have strong feelings about it, one of the many ways of sharing and being close at this difficult time is to talk it over together. Whatever decision may be made—and finally, this must be left to the adults —talking about how each person feels brings you closer to one another.

Sometimes the parent who has died had strong feelings about this matter and the remaining parent wants to carry out his or her partner's wishes. These

are certainly decisions that are much too compli-
cated and difficult to involve very little children.

Terry's father was a doctor. In a letter attached
to his will he had written that when he died, he
wanted his body given to the hospital where he had
worked. If any of his organs could be used in
transplants, he wanted this to be done. He left his
corneas to an eye bank. All of this was very hard
on his wife and three children, but they wanted to
fulfill his wishes. The memorial service that was
held was to comfort them, to help them face the
fact of his death, to help them share their grief
with others. But they obeyed his wishes about his
body.

Some people prefer to be buried in the ground,
others prefer cremation, in which the body is
burned and only the ashes are buried. Some people
feel very strongly that a coffin should be left open
so that loved ones can say a last good-by. Other
people feel that the body in the coffin is not the
person as they want to remember him or her.

All of these questions are very real and important;
they are a part of the fact of death. We can bear
them if we face them openly and honestly together,
without being ashamed of our feelings, and without
being afraid to say how we feel.

Some children want to see the dead parent in
the coffin because what they imagine may be so
much worse than what is real. Other children may

be terrified of seeing a dead person. To make your decision you need to think hard about how you feel and what will make you the least uncomfortable. In the long run, the important part is letting your feelings help you reach a decision. What sometimes happens is that grownups think it would be a terrible experience, but you don't feel that way. Or maybe they think it would be a good idea, but you don't want to look. Let them know how you feel. Later on you will begin to recognize that the important memories you will keep forever have to do with the time when your father or mother was alive, not when he or she was already dead.

At first, however, it is not at all unusual for a child to think quite a lot about what happens to a dead person after he or she is buried. It may be very difficult for a parent to answer your questions, but a close relative or your family doctor might be willing to sit down and answer your questions. It ought to be someone who can give you an accurate and simple explanation of the physical effects of death. Perhaps the nurse at school or the biology teacher. And more and more often these days, funeral directors are people who care very much about helping families in many ways. Sometimes they know a lot about the feelings we have after someone we love dies. When you meet each other you will probably be able to tell if this is someone you feel like talking to.

One of the things we know through the experiences of many parents and children is that it is better to have *all* our questions answered, no matter how difficult the answer may be.

When Allen was seven years old, his mother, who had been pregnant for six months, gave birth to a premature baby who only lived a few hours. Allen's parents decided to have the baby cremated. Because he had lived for such a brief time they did not want to have a funeral service.

When Allen's mother came home from the hospital, she told him that the baby had been too tiny and weak to live. She did not say anything about what had happened to the baby's body, and Allen was too shy to ask. His mother and father thought that telling him the baby had been cremated would upset him too much.

A few weeks later, Allen began to feel afraid of going to school. He was afraid of the dark and wanted a light on in his room all night. He began to be afraid of opening a closet door or opening a dresser drawer. It got so bad that he began throwing up every morning when it was time to go to school. Allen didn't understand what was happening to him. His mother and father didn't know what to do, so they went to talk to the school psychologist. She told them that perhaps Allen needed to talk about the death of the baby—to know more about what had happened. The next day Allen's father took him for a ride in the car. There was a cemetery near a church in their town. His father stopped the car and began to talk about the sad thing that had happened. He told Allen how he and his mother had cried together in the hospital. He said, "I guess we should have let you know how sad we were, so you could have been sad with us." Then Allen asked what had been done with the baby's body, and his father told him about burial and cremation. Allen said, "I thought the baby was somewhere in the house." When he said that, he realized why he had been so afraid of opening the closet door or the dresser drawers. His father told him exactly what had happened—the baby's ashes had been buried. Allen felt relieved. Later he and his parents cried together about the baby. His mother and father realized that what Allen had imagined was worse than the truth.

Each family has its own special and different ideas about funerals. Each religion has different funeral services. Most people now agree that whatever these differences in ideas and beliefs and customs may be, all of us need some way in which to share our grief with those we love. A funeral is a special time to say good-by and to feel close to others.

There are also many different ideas about what happens to people after they are dead. Many people believe in an afterlife when the soul of the dead person goes to heaven. Other people believe that the person goes on living through his or her children, through accomplishments, or through memories left behind. Many other people feel that life and death are still great mysteries they cannot fully understand.

Each family gains comfort from their shared beliefs—each in their own special way. But there are also many experiences we all share at such times.

GRIEVING:
THE FEELINGS
WE SHARE

During the first stage of grief, most people just cannot accept the fact that someone they love has really died. You hope for some magic to happen; you want desperately to believe it's all just a bad dream. But it isn't.

Several years ago a friend of mine died. Almost a year after his death, I still sometimes had dreams of sitting in his office, talking to him. In one very clear dream he said, "Don't believe it, Eda, I didn't die." I woke up and for one instant I felt happy and relieved. These are very painful dreams to wake up from, but they are a normal part of mourning. In dreams we often wish for things we cannot have.

Jenny's mother died when Jenny was ten years old. During the first few months after her mother's death Jenny dreamed about her mother almost every night. Waking up and realizing she had just been dreaming hurt Jenny so much that she began to wish the dreams would go away.

About a year later she met another girl at school whose mother had just died. They became friends, partly because they understood each other's feelings so well. Jenny asked Audrey if she dreamed about her mother and Audrey said no, she never had. When Jenny got home from school that day, she told her father, "It's a funny thing; when Audrey told me she never dreamed about her mother, I felt sorry for her. Right after Mommy died, I dreamt about her so much, it was like I was keeping her near me for a while longer."

Sometimes dreams help us to bear what is almost unbearable. At least during the dream we can feel happy again.

MEMORIES: FADING IN AND FADING OUT

Right after a parent dies, many children are able to see him or her very clearly in their minds. They can even remember how their mother's bath powder smelled or their father's shaving lotion. It is easy to remember what a hug felt like, to have Mom's arms around you, or to remember what it felt like to sit in Dad's lap. Painful as these memories may be, they are also comforting.

But after a while a very scary thing happens; you *can't* remember, no matter how hard you try. Sometimes this happens in a few months, sometimes not for a year or longer. But sooner or later it happens to most people, and when it does it may make you feel more sad and lonely than ever.

Losing these memories seems to happen at about the same time you begin really to accept the death. You go through a period of change. Something inside you is getting ready to let go of your parent. After a while you begin to remember again, even more clearly sometimes. It is as if a special kind of "good-by" is going on, and when you have passed through this stage, you begin to remember again. The difference is that often now what you remember most clearly are *feelings* rather than faces or smells or touches. You remember things like gentleness or joking; arguments and making up, shared hobbies and trips, feeling homesick for Mom at a sleep-away camp; feeling so good to be sleeping in your own room again when she came in to kiss you good night.

THE HARDEST TIME OF ALL

Gradually the time comes when you begin really to understand that your mother or father will never come back. This is usually months after his or her death. At first, you may wonder why you are crying harder and more often now than right after it happened. That seems strange. Actually it is very natural and makes good sense. You have had time to become stronger and more able to face the fact that never, ever again will you be with your parent as you were before his or her death.

WHAT'S GOING TO HAPPEN TO ME?

When you begin to accept the idea that a parent is not going to come back, it is natural to become very frightened. And with the fears about who will take care of you, you may begin to feel very angry. This can be very confusing—how can you feel so angry at someone you love and need so much?

Anger is a normal feeling. Sooner or later it happens to every child who loses a parent. Grownups have the very same kinds of feelings. You may find yourself thinking, "How could Daddy leave me if he really loved me?" Or wonder, "Didn't Mommy care what happens to me?" You may feel that you have been deserted and that makes you very, very angry—even though you may know perfectly well that your parent could not help getting sick or being in an accident. Feelings sometimes have little or nothing to do with the facts.

But feeling angry usually makes us feel guilty. You may think, "What an awful person I am to be so angry." You are not an awful person at all. It is natural to feel angry when you have been hurt.

Josh was nine years old when his father died. His dad had been sick for a long time and had to stay home from work. Because he felt so sick, he sometimes lost patience with Josh. When Josh made a lot of noise or talked back to his mother, or had to be nagged to do his homework, his father would get very exasperated, and once he even said, "You'll be the death of me!"

After his father died, Josh kept remembering that sentence. In addition to feeling angry that his father had left him, he also had the feeling that it was his fault that his father had died. If he had been more considerate, quieter, more obedient, maybe his father would not have died.

Grownups often say things they don't mean, especially when they are angry, tired, or upset—just the way children do. Josh's father was just using an expression that many parents use without thinking. No one can really expect a child to be quiet and thoughtful all the time. Even a person who is sick knows that children are neither "good" nor "bad," but just young and human and bound to get noisy some of the time.

Most parents can understand your angry feelings because they feel the same way. You may already have heard your mother crying and saying something like, "Damn it, how could Larry leave me with two children to raise?" Your mother doesn't really mean what she is saying any more than you do. When we are hurting so much, we sometimes need to get angry about it.

A FEELING THAT LOVING IS DANGEROUS

An idea which may come into your mind is that if you had not loved your mother or father so much, you would not be so miserable now that he or she has died. Maybe it is better just not to love anybody too much! You begin to feel you don't love anyone anymore. When a sister or a brother wants to crawl into bed with you so you can comfort each other, you kick him or her out. When your favorite uncle wants to take you to a football game, you may say you don't want to go. When Grandma wants you to sit on her lap, you squirm away. Part of you wants comforting so much, but another part of you says, "Keep away, everybody! If I love you or need too much, you might also leave me, too!"

Feeling that love is dangerous is a natural reaction to the pain of mourning, but it will not last forever, unless you try to hide it. Knowing you have such feelings, and accepting them, will help them pass. Loving and being loved are the most important parts of being a human being; without them, life is not worth living.

You have had to learn, at a very early age, what some people don't understand until they have become much older—that pain is a part of life, and must be accepted if joy is also going to be a part of one's life. We need love in order to live. Sometimes that need will lead to suffering—but it will also lead to the greatest happiness that is possible.

THE FEAR OF LOSING THE PARENT WHO IS STILL ALIVE

The greatest fear of all—and the most natural one —is that something terrible might happen to the parent you still have. This may start right away, because the parent who is left may be so grief-stricken, so unable to help you, that you may feel you have already been abandoned by *both* parents. Your mother or father seems a million miles away— curled up in bed, crying, hiding in the bathroom, taking sleeping pills or tranquilizers the doctor has prescribed, which make your mother or father groggy and seem far away. Doctors often do this because they feel that if they can help their patient get through the first weeks without too much loss of sleep and with some relief from hurting feelings, he or she will be able to cope with life sooner, become stronger and better able to help his or her children.

But you may feel left out and alone, and that makes you worry even more. Beth became terrified when her father had to take an airplane trip; maybe the plane would crash. Jonathan became more and more upset every time his mother took a cigarette; maybe smoking would give her lung cancer and she would die, too. Jean and Bob became very worried when their mother went back to work after their dad died. She had to get up at six o'clock in the morning, travel an hour each way to and from the city, do all the shopping and cooking and cleaning. Maybe she would get sick and die, too.

Such fears are natural, but as life goes on they will become less frequent and less strong. You will realize that people must go on living their lives, and while it is certainly wise to take reasonable precautions, it is impossible to be 100 percent safe. Slowly but surely everyone in the family will begin to find a sensible balance between caution and necessary activities. Beth's father had to travel in his job, but when Jonathan's mother realized how he felt about her smoking, she realized that he was right. Difficult as it was, she gradually stopped smoking. Jean and Bob were able to realize after a few months that their mother needed to be busy—that she really loved her work, didn't mind the traveling, and that housework helped her to pass the evenings when she felt most lonely for their father.

Another thing which makes children worry about the parent who is still alive is that sometimes he or she says something that is pretty frightening. A mother or a father may be crying and say to a relative or friend, "I just can't go on alone. I wish I could die too!" If you overhear such a statement, you may feel both scared and angry. But you can be quite sure your parent does not mean what he or she is saying. This is another of those statements that just come out when a person is hurting a lot.

You may also overhear a parent say, "I wish we'd never had any children!" Or "I wish I could run away." Or a parent may say directly, "Can't you leave me alone—I have enough troubles without you driving me crazy!" Now you feel as if you have been deserted by two parents. It seems more than you can bear.

If you are aware of how you are feeling, it will help if you can understand what is happening to your mother or father. He or she is expressing his or her grief—and very similar feelings of desertion —by saying things they don't really mean. Also, children are a constant reminder of the parent who has died. Maybe you look very much like your father or mother. Just seeing you and your brothers and sisters reminds a husband or a wife of all the love and happiness he or she once had. Sometimes the pain is so great that the living parent has a momentary wish not to be reminded every minute, and so there may be outbursts of this kind. Remember: just as you will begin to recover from your grief, so will your mother or father. Within a few months he or she will gradually stop feeling so bad. Then Mom or Dad will be *so glad* to have you as a part of a husband or wife they need never lose completely because you were born.

FEELING ANGRY AT THE LIVING PARENT

Danny was having a fight with his mother. He wanted to take his lunch to school in a paper bag instead of a lunchbox. The other kids in his class teased him and said a lunch box was for "mama's

babies." His mother said the food might spoil and that it was too dangerous to carry a thermos bottle that way. Suddenly Danny screamed, "I wish *you* had died instead of Daddy! *He* didn't treat me like a baby!" Both he and his mother looked at each other in shocked silence. His mother became very quiet and Danny felt terribly guilty for what he had said. Both Danny and his mother need to understand that such a scene is very normal and happens to most people in families where one parent has died.

When a parent dies, we soon begin to forget the unhappy times—the times when that parent got angry at us, wouldn't let us do what we wanted, nagged at us, made us feel stupid, or was very impatient with us. You may begin to think to yourself, "Dad never yelled at me about those things—I wish Mom had died instead," or "Daddy is just no good at taking care of me when I feel sick—it would have been better if my Mom had lived and Daddy died." Or some children think that "If Mom had died instead of Dad we wouldn't have to worry about money so much, because he got paid more."

There is no reason to feel frightened or ashamed when you have thoughts about wishing the parent who lived had died instead. When you miss someone terribly, you begin to have a dream picture of that person. He or she becomes more beautiful or handsome, more kind and gentle, more understanding than he or she really was. It is nice to remember the happy times when you were having fun, when you felt most loved.

It is perfectly natural to want to remember the best times, and we should. But we also need to remember that neither parent was ever all-good, all-wise, or all-wonderful, just as we are not like that. The living parent has to be fully responsible for the child. He or she must discipline the child according to his or her beliefs. And since daily living is full of everyday problems, it is natural to wish these might have been avoided if the other parent had died instead. Actually, you probably realize that things would not have been much better at all—just different.

There are some cases, however, where some of these thoughts are based on facts. Richard's father was run over by a taxi. Richard became more upset as time went on. After three or four months, he was afraid of just about everything. He cried more and more. He had very frightening nightmares. He couldn't do any of his schoolwork. His teacher called his mother in for a conference. His mother did not want to come, but when she finally did come to school, the teacher realized she had been drinking very heavily. She had been an alcoholic long before Richard's father died. She often screamed and threw things, and Richard had been afraid of her for a long time. She was a person who was very troubled in her feelings and had not received any help.

Richard's teacher helped his mother realize they both needed help. She recommended a child-guidance clinic where there are special people who know how to help with troubled feelings. When Richard was helped to understand that his feelings about wishing his mother had died instead of his father were not so silly, he began to be less afraid. His father had been a shy and quiet man very much like Richard. They had understood each other very well. They had both worried about Richard's mother, but had not been able to help her.

In situations like Richard's what usually happens is that a child learns to turn to other people for help. In Richard's case, however, his mother began to realize just how important she now was to Richard, and she was able to get help she herself had needed for a long time. A death in the family can often help a troubled and unhappy parent begin to face his or her problems. If that does not happen, other people—grandparents, uncles and aunts, neighbors, a minister or doctor, the people at school —can begin to step in and help.

Anger at the parent who is still alive—whatever the circumstances—becomes less strong as time goes by. You will begin to feel strong enough to go on with your own life as you begin to enjoy learning and playing, being with friends and family. It just takes time.

WORRYING ABOUT YOURSELF

Judy woke up one morning with a terrible stomachache. She felt weak and dizzy and when she tried to eat her breakfast, she felt like throwing up. She was very frightened, because those were the very symptoms her father had when he first got sick, before he died. She was so scared that she couldn't tell her mother how sick she felt.

She went to school and tried to pretend there was nothing wrong, but after a little while she had to go to the nurse's office, where she began to cry. She finally told the nurse she was afraid she was going to die, too. The nurse gave her a big hug. Then she took her temperature. It was 102°. The nurse said, "Judy dear, you have the flu—just like four other children in your class! Lots of sicknesses have the same symptoms, at least at first. Your daddy had cancer of the stomach, which is a very serious disease. You will be feeling fine after you have been in bed for a few days and taken some medicine. I'll call your mother at her office and then I guess your baby-sitter will come and take you home in a taxi. You are *not* going to die!"

There was nothing silly about the way Judy felt. When someone you love very much gets sick and dies, it is very natural to worry about dying yourself. For a while it may be something you just can't stop thinking about.

Rachel's father was killed in a car accident. Every time Rachel had to get into a car, she was terrified that there would be another crash and she would be killed. When the feelings got very bad, she told her mother how she felt. Her mother said, "You know, I get the same feeling sometimes. But I can't see any way we can go on living here if we don't travel by car, and I think we'll get over it more quickly if we just do what we have to do. For a while we won't take any long trips. Until we begin to get over this feeling, we'll just go to the store and to school and do the things we have to do."

Rachel felt better because she could share this feeling with her mother. She didn't feel ashamed of it anymore. The feeling began to go away, and she was surprised when she heard herself saying, a few months later, "Hey, Mom, when can we go out to that ranch where they let you go horseback riding? It's not so far—only about three hours' driving."

THE FEAR OF BEING LEFT ALL ALONE

At one time or another all children have the fear that something might happen to both parents and they might be alone with no one to take care of them. When a parent dies this fear becomes stronger.

One thing you can be absolutely certain about— *you will never be left alone.* All children need to know that they will have someone to take care of them until they are old enough to take care of themselves. Sometimes your parents may have made you feel like a baby and that made you angry. At the same time you also know that you are not old enough to take care of yourself, that you need grownups to help you grow up.

If anything were ever to happen to your second parent, there will be people who love you very much and will take care of you. Your grandparents, your aunts and uncles, your parents' closest friends will never, ever leave you. What you may not know is that most parents make out a will which states who is to care for their children if they were both to die at the same time. Most parents discuss this matter very seriously. They usually choose another family—it can be either friends or relatives—whom they feel would bring up their children the way they want them to be raised. Then they go and talk to the other couple. Often two couples will agree that they will exchange this responsibility. If you are frightened and wonder about this, you can talk to your mother or father about it. You will probably be relieved to learn that ever since you were born your parents have considered this matter very carefully. The chances of losing both your parents is very, very slight, but every child wants to know he or she will be loved and cared for if this should ever happen.

WHEN THE MOURNING IS OVER BEFORE IT BEGINS

Lester's father died when Lester was ten years old. Lester is now a grown man, and he remembers that when his father died, he just could not cry. He could not feel sad. He told me, "I remember that I pretended to cry and feel bad at the funeral, but I really wasn't feeling anything. At the same time I thought there was something seriously the matter with me. But I realized much later when I was already an adult that my mourning was over when my father died. I knew for more than a year after he had a very serious heart attack that he was going to die. I remember overhearing a conversation between two of my uncles. Then I went for a walk along a beach and sat down on the dunes, hiding in the tall grass, and sobbed for hours. I did that several times. I think what happened to me was that I had been saying good-by to my father for many months before he actually died. All the feelings of grief were already spent by the time of his death."

If a parent is very ill for a long time it is more than likely that a great deal of the mourning has already occurred before a parent dies. That may very well account for some of the numb and empty feelings a child may have.

A FEELING OF RELIEF

One kind of feeling may surprise you very much— a feeling of relief. This is not at all uncommon; it is just part of being human. Yet it makes many parents and children feel more guilty and ashamed than any other feeling.

David was eleven years old when his father died. His father was very tall and strong and athletic. He played football in high school and college, and from the time David was about three years old his dad had tried to teach him how to play baseball. David was more like his mother. He was kind of skinny and clumsy and he just wasn't interested in the kinds of things his father enjoyed most. He liked reading and music most of all. Before his father got sick, David often felt very angry at his father, who kept pushing him and pushing him in sports activities. David felt like a failure, and that feeling made him sad and angry. When his father died, David felt relieved for one brief moment. At least now he didn't have to worry about disappointing his father and he wouldn't have to spend so much of his time doing things he hated.

There is nothing terrible about such thoughts. David also knew that he loved his father and that there were times when they had enjoyed each other's company a lot. His father had just been teaching him to play ragtime on the piano. When they did that, David felt warm waves of love and happiness as he sat next to his father on the piano bench. Loving and hating feelings are part of every important relationship. No matter how much you will miss a parent who has died, there are bound to be some unhappy memories of not getting along with each other, and being relieved that that part is over.

Laurie's mother was sick for two whole years before she died. During that time Laurie and her two younger brothers had a very hard time. Laurie was only seven when her mother had to be in bed most of the time. The boys were two and five. Laurie's mother began to change—she cried a lot and couldn't stand any noise in the house, and after a while she didn't even seem to want to see the children very much. Laurie was frightened and she was also angry. Her parents began to expect her to take care of herself and her brothers. She had too little time to play with her own friends. Her father was so worried and busy taking care of her mother that she missed the wonderful times she had spent with him alone, before her mother got sick.

When Laurie's mother finally died, Laurie felt relieved. She was so glad it was over at last—the long illness that had been so hard on everyone in the family. She was glad her mother's suffering was over too. But then she began to remember how much she had loved her mother, how happy they were before she got sick. She was shocked and ashamed, knowing a part of her was relieved it was all over.

People often do change a great deal when they are very sick. Even if they don't, it is very painful for a child to live with a parent who can't always act like a parent anymore. It is natural for children to want their parents to take care of them, not the other way around.

If David and Laurie had been too ashamed of their feelings to even let themselves know they were having them, they might have become even more upset than they already were. Knowing that loving and hating feelings happen in every family can help us to feel our sadness more deeply—and doing that is an important part of beginning to feel better.

WANTING TO CHANGE THINGS—QUICKLY

Joan's father had only been dead two months when she began to have thoughts that made her feel very confused and ashamed. She wanted her mother to get married again—right away! She found herself looking at the men teachers in her school and wondering if they were married. She remembered that the wife of her pediatrician had died several years before and she wished he would ask her mother for a date. When her mother went to a dinner party where she was to meet a divorced man who was the brother of a neighbor, Joan began daydreaming about his being very nice and marrying her mother.

She could not understand how she could be having such thoughts. She loved her father and missed him so much—why did she want to "replace" him so soon? Yet these feelings are really not at all hard to understand. If you have been happy before, you want to be happy again. Men and women who have been happily married and then widowed are often interested in marrying again. They know how wonderful a marriage can be.

It is natural for a young child to want and need a mother and a father. It felt so good when that's the way it was! Wanting a new mother or father is actually a great compliment to the parent who has died. It is a sign of just how important that person was and how hard it is to live without a mother and father.

Another reason for such feelings is that you think that maybe a new parent will help you forget the sadness. Memories hurt so much, and sometimes you wish you could just stop feeling so miserable. Unfortunately, it just doesn't work that way. It is important to experience sad feelings for quite a long time. Then, when they begin to go away, they stay away for longer and longer periods of time. If we are too impatient and try to push them away too fast, they may come back much stronger later on.

This first impulse to have your parent remarry quickly usually happens while the pain is still very great. Later on, when things have settled down and life seems more normal, many children begin to resent the idea of a remarriage. By then, they may look on everyone a parent dates as an intruder.

Some children want the family to move right after a parent dies. They just cannot bear to be reminded every second of how things once were. Often the worst times are coming home after being

away for a vacation. For a while a child may have forgotten. Coming back to the house brings back all the most painful memories.

Beth says, "Every place I look in this house, I see my daddy. I just wish we could move, leave all the furniture and everything, and go to a new school and a new city. Then I could forget." This may seem like a good idea, but it doesn't usually work out too well. It is a kind of shortcut that doesn't allow feelings to happen the way they need to happen.

Difficult as it is, most people begin to recover from a death more easily if they don't try to push away their memories. This is called "the work of mourning." When something terribly sad has happened to us we need to feel that sadness for a long, long time. What usually happens is that during the first few months there are awful waves of pain that make us cry a lot. Then, slowly but surely, these waves begin to come less often. They are just as intense and painful when they happen, but after a while they may come once or twice a week, then once or twice a month. They never go away completely—there is bound to be a permanent scar—but the wound does heal.

MOURNING IN YOUR OWN SPECIAL WAY

When Ben's father died, Ben was numb; he didn't know what to do. The house was full of relatives, but nobody was paying any attention to him. He tried to think what he could do that would have made his father happy. He remembered that he and his father had been working on a bookshelf in their basement shop and he thought to himself, "Wouldn't he be proud of me if I could finish it all by myself!" He ran downstairs and began to hammer.

All of a sudden he heard his mother yelling at him from the top of the basement stairs. She was saying, "Haven't you any *feelings?* Your father isn't even buried yet—and you're playing!" Ben is a grown man now, but he never forgot how terrible he felt. He had thought he was doing something to show how much he loved his father—and it had been completely misunderstood.

People have their own individual ways of expressing grief. Sometimes, if someone else doesn't understand this, you may have to explain it. Or, you may have to try to understand someone else. Karen was shocked when she heard her mother playing records of musicals just a few days after her father died. How could anyone listen to gay, light-hearted songs at such a time? Well, those were musicals her mother and father had gone to, long before Karen was born. Her mother was remembering those happy times.

Some people need to take long walks alone; other people want to have lots of company. Some people need to be very quiet; others need loud music. One person will feel like looking through all the family scrapbooks; another person will want to put them on the highest shelf in the closet for a long, long time.

During the early weeks and months of grief we need to respect our own needs and the feelings of others in our family. There is no "right" or "wrong" way to feel. The important thing is for each person to find what is best for him or herself.

RECOVERING
FROM GRIEF

⚜

Marilyn is eleven years old. Her mother died eight
months ago. Marilyn *never* mentions her mother.
Her father tells a friend, "I guess Marilyn has forgotten her mother."

Nothing could be farther from the truth. Marilyn
is still suffering so much that she just cannot bring
herself to mention anything she remembers. The
problem is that Marilyn's mother committed suicide.
Her death was no accident. It was Marilyn who had
found her mother after she had taken all the sleeping pills. Under such circumstances it is natural for
a child to suffer so much that she just cannot bear
her own feelings; they become deeply buried in her
mind. She doesn't really even know they are there.
But she feels kind of paralyzed.

Covering up feelings doesn't mean they have gone away. Marilyn will continue to suffer in one way or another unless she can unlock those feelings. In her case her mother's death was such a shock that she may need special help to recover. She may need to go and talk to a special person who understands a great deal about problems in feelings. Never being able to talk about a parent who has died is not a sign that you have gotten over his or her death. It means there are unhappy feelings interfering with remembering.

When a parent commits suicide it is very hard for a child to believe that this death, like most others, was caused by an illness. And yet that is exactly the case. Some people get sick mostly in their bodies, some sick mostly in their feelings. When a person ends his or her own life, it means that they were too upset in their feelings to go on living. It does *not* mean that he or she did not love his or her family. A person who dies because of un-happy feelings is just as "sick" as someone who dies from a disease like multiple sclerosis. Marilyn's mother really had no control over her illness. It is possible that if Marilyn can be helped to under-stand this, her own feelings won't hurt so much and she may begin to be able to talk about her mother and remember her.

Some people have the opposite problem—they can't forget the parent who died. Barbara, aged twelve, seems to have built a little shrine to her daddy's memory in her room. She has about fifty pictures of him on one wall of her room. She has his baseball glove, his pipe, his high-school ring, and the glass paperweight from his office desk on her dresser. Almost every day she plays tapes of the whole family talking and joking so she can hear her father's voice. Every weekend she pleads with her mother to show her some of the home movies they have. Her father loved the opera and Barbara has asked everyone to give her opera records for Christmas and her birthday, and she plays them whenever she's at home, lying on her bed with her eyes closed. She hardly ever plays with other children anymore. She insists upon going to the public tennis courts a few times every week because her father was teaching her to play tennis just before he died. Her grandmother—her father's mother—tells her mother, "I don't see what you are worrying about—I think it's wonderful that Barbara loved Joe so much and is keeping his memory alive."

Spending all one's time remembering is as much of a problem as not wanting to remember at all. In Barbara's case, things were not always so wonderful while her father was still alive. She has an older brother whom her father adored—much more than he cared for her. She had been sure of that. He just seemed to like boys better. Barbara had tried to like the same things—baseball and tennis and so on—but mostly her father and Bill went off together, leaving her behind. She had found out that she could get her father's attention if she acted as if she liked going to an opera. Her happiest times were the two or three times he had taken Barbara to see and hear an opera. She didn't understand what was happening onstage, and it all seemed pretty silly and boring, but she was so glad that her father was sitting next to her and paying attention to her. Most of the time, though, she felt unloved and left out.

Barbara is manufacturing a relationship which never really existed while her father was still alive Here in her room, with all her mementos, she is having the close relationship with her dad that she had always dreamed of but which had never really happened.

Both Marilyn and Barbara are behaving in ways that will not be helpful to them in the long run. Each one has special problems which are interfering with their recovering from the blow of a parent's dying.

Mark, on the other hand, seems to be going through a process which is helping him to go on with his life. He and his mom can joke and laugh about some of the crazy things they remember his dad doing many years before, when they were all happy together. There was the time his father had set fire to the tent when they were camping because he didn't know how to light the lantern. There was the time he fell into a lake, trying to catch Mark's runaway toy sailboat. They also talk about some sad times. Toward the end of his life, Mark's father kept losing his jobs. Mark knew that his mother and father had many fights and he knew they had talked about getting a divorce.

Mark feels it is O.K. to ask his mother any questions he wants to, and she answers as honestly as she can. She told him, "Mark darling, Daddy was still a little boy in some ways. He could be so funny and so wonderful! People always had a good time when he was around. But he just never grew up altogether and he wasn't strong enough to take care of a family. It was very hard for him to work and he had trouble keeping a job. It was a sad thing and it led to many problems, but you and I know he had some wonderful qualities."

Mark spends a lot of time with his aunts and uncles and grandparents. He belongs to several after-school clubs. He takes a special course in astronomy on Saturday mornings because he is so fascinated by this subject. He can remember and talk about good times and bad times—and most of all, he is going on living his life very fully. He is recovering.

Mark's father wasn't the least bit interested in astronomy. Mark wants to study that for himself.

This is the most important part of beginning to recover from the death of a parent—doing the things that make *you* feel good, living *your* own life.

NEEDING OTHER PEOPLE: GROWNUPS

Of course leading your own life isn't something you can do alone. Other people are very important. One of the problems that may come up during the months of recovering is that you are not sure how to talk to other people—you feel shy. Something has happened which has changed your life completely and you wonder how this will affect your relationships with both grownups and children.

Sarah's father died eight months ago. She is ten years old. She is a friend of mine, and when she came to visit me recently, I asked her if there were any special problems that had come up that she and I had not thought about before. She said, "Yes, there is one thing that I didn't know was going to happen—I never know whom to tell that my daddy is dead."

We both realized how important this was. Right after Sarah's father died, she told everyone about it. She wanted and needed as much sympathy and comfort as she could get. Most people had been very kind. Some grownups made so much of a fuss over her that she would begin to wish she hadn't told them. A few children had been awful. There was a girl in her class at school who said "So what?" when Sarah said her father was dead. Sarah had gotten very upset and had cried. Later her mother explained that some children get mean when they really feel scared. She said, "Probably hearing what had happened to you made Gerry wonder if that same thing might happen to her. She got angry at you for making her worry about that and so she acted in a cruel way. It's too bad when that happens, but it can't be helped."

After the early weeks or months of mourning, Sarah told me, you begin to wonder when it is appropriate to mention your parent's death and when it is not. She gave me some examples. During the second half of the school year a new gym teacher had come to her school. Sarah is a little plump and not very athletic. She hates team sports because in her school the class elects the team captains and then they choose their teams. She is often chosen last. This has been very painful, but Sarah tries hard not to show how upset she gets.

One day, with the new gym teacher, she just burst into tears in the middle of the choosing. The day before had been her father's birthday and she was more upset than she had been for several months. The teacher was impatient with her. "It's just a game," she said. "It's not worth getting hysterical about it." Sarah wanted the teacher to understand how she felt, but she felt shy about telling her. She felt the other children would think she was asking for special favors. She didn't say anything.

My idea was that there are times when a person needs to know why a child is upset. I suggested to Sarah that if she didn't want to tell someone in front of other children, maybe she could have waited after class and explained why that day was especially hard for her.

At another time, Sarah went to Elsa's house to play after school. She was surprised to find another girl there—a child who had just moved next door to her friend. Sarah and Elsa had been friends for a long time. Suddenly Sarah felt she was being pushed aside. She felt very upset and began to cry. She said, "Elsa, it's very mean of you not to be nice to me when you know I have no father!" Elsa looked very shocked and embarrassed. For the rest of the afternoon, nobody had a good time.

In this case, I told Sarah maybe it had not been such a good idea to bring up her father's death. All children go through periods of competition over "best friends." It is a natural part of growing up. Sometimes you are "in" and sometimes you are "out," and in the process all the children are learning more about getting along with others—about likes and dislikes, about feelings. Maybe in that case, Sarah was trying to use her loss to gain an unfair advantage.

We decided it was very hard to know when to say something and when not to. One just had to live through a lot of situations for a while and learn what helped and what didn't help. Sarah told me, "You find out which people will make you feel better and which people make you feel worse. I told one girl I didn't know very well about my daddy's dying and she was wonderful. She said her parents were divorced, and we talked all afternoon about how each of us felt. She tried to understand me and I tried to understand her. Then another time, I told a boy I met at day camp. I could see I upset him a lot. He never talked to me again. Some children are too sensitive and you are better off not talking to them. It's the same with grownups. You just can't tell ahead of time."

It is important not to become discouraged when things don't work out too well. This is a time in your life when it is natural and necessary for you to lean on other people, to need help. There is no reason to feel ashamed or shy about that. Nancy was eight years old when her father died. Her school was close enough to her house so that she had always gone home for lunch. But now when she went home, her mother wasn't there—she had gone back to work. Nancy was very scared of going into the empty house. The kids in school often joked about ghosts and haunted houses and she was frightened she might really see the ghost of her father. She felt it was silly, but she just couldn't help it.

Besides that, the house was just too lonely. The silence reminded her of how she missed her father. When she told her mother that she wanted to stay in school and eat lunch there, her mother said, "Nancy, that's silly. It's too expensive. And anyway, all you have to do is take your lunch out of the refrigerator."

One day Nancy's aunt came to visit. When she and Nancy were alone, Nancy began to cry. There were a lot of things bothering her. She didn't want to come home for lunch, but she felt guilty about asking her mother for the lunch money when her mother had to work to take care of them now. She was scared that her mother was thinking about moving to a smaller house in another town. She was also upset because her mother was gone all day, even when Nancy got home from school.

Nancy's aunt thought maybe she should have a talk with Carol, Nancy's mother. Probably Carol had so much on her own mind that she just wasn't listening carefully enough to Nancy's fears. And, as soon as Carol understood how upset Nancy really was, she began to make new arrangements. She realized that at least for a while, until Nancy felt better, she would have to spend some extra money on school lunches and baby-sitters. She told her sister, "I guess I just wasn't thinking. It seemed crazy to let Nancy stay in school for lunch when she knows perfectly well how to do it herself, and I couldn't see much point in a baby-sitter after school because Nancy goes to all kinds of activities after school—but I guess she's still hurting too much and needs some extra reassurances for a while."

It isn't being babyish at all if you feel you need more care, more help from grownups, after a parent has died. The shock has shaken you up so much that you may need to go back to feeling and being younger and more dependent, at least for a little while.

One parent can't be two parents, no matter how hard he or she may try. A mother can't be a father and a father can't be a mother. You need other grownups to help make up to you in some ways for not having a mother or a father.

Peggy's mother died just before Peggy's twelfth birthday. Several months later Peggy told her father that she needed to buy her first bra. She felt shy and embarrassed. Her father didn't want Peggy to feel deserted, so he decided to take her shopping himself. She also needed a party dress and her mother had promised she could get a pair of clogs. The shopping trip was a disaster. Peggy was shy and uncomfortable and her dad got tired and bored. It wasn't any fun at all for either of them. Peggy decided this wasn't going to work at all. She finally got up enough courage to tell her Aunt Florence, whom she loved a lot, what had happened, and to ask if she'd go with her the next time. Aunt Florence was delighted. She said, "As a matter of fact, Peggy, I've been meaning to talk to you. There are times in a young woman's life when she really wants to talk to another woman. I hope you know I love you and that I want you to come and talk to me anytime you want."

Frank and his father loved to go camping together. On the first trip, Frank's mother had gone along and it was terrible. She hated every minute of it! "My ancestors would have given anything to have hot running water and indoor plumbing," she said. "Why should I give it up?" She just didn't understand anything about the special joys of outdoor living and roughing it.

When Frank's father died, a big part of Frank's sadness had to do with missing the camping trips. His grandfather offered to go with him, but Frank knew he didn't really want to. His only uncle lived too far away. He went on one trip with a school friend and his family, but it wasn't the same at all; he felt like an outsider.

One night he was discussing this with his baby-sitter, a high-school girl. Usually he didn't talk to her much—he was angry that his mother still thought he needed a sitter. But one night her boyfriend called her on the phone and Frank heard them talking about a camping trip their church was sponsoring. Frank told the baby-sitter how much he loved camping and she said, "Let me ask our minister; all the kids are much older than you are, but maybe you could go along anyway. I think he's taking his own son who is about your age." It turned out fine. Even though Frank belonged to a different religion and a different church, he and the minister and his son became good friends and camping partners.

Sometimes it takes quite a while to find the kind of person or people you need, but it can be done. There are always at least a few people you can turn to. The librarian in Helen's school is also a neighbor, and she's a real friend. Jim goes to talk to the man who owns the delicatessen on Main Street, where his father used to go to talk. Charlie confides in his married older sister. Sometimes we get the help we need from old friends, sometimes we make new friends—mostly it's a combination of both.

Often the most normal grownup friends turn out to be the relatives of the dead parent. After all, you are the most important part of what is left of your parent, and especially precious to them. Sometimes this works out very well—but not always. Your father's or mother's relatives may be people you never really knew that well; maybe you never even liked them very much. Your family may not have had much to do with them for many years. It is important to remember that forcing a relationship just because it *seems* logical doesn't work well at all.

Sometimes a husband or a wife may not get along too well with their spouse's family. Things may appear to be all right on the surface but you may have heard your parents arguing about each other's in-laws. Or sometimes things may have happened to cause bad feelings for a long time.

Eric's mother was polite to her husband's family when they visited while Eric's father was alive, but she resented them very much. When Eric's father told his family he was going to marry Eric's mother, his dad's family had been very upset; they thought it was a terrible mistake—that she wasn't the right person for him. Eric's mother had never forgiven them. When her husband died, and while she was still in a state of shock, Eric had heard her say, "Well at least now I never have to see Paul's rotten relatives again!"

Eric felt badly about this. He wanted to see his grandparents and his uncles and aunts because they reminded him of his dad. He knew they loved him too. His father's family tried for a while to make peace with Eric's mother. After all, they said, we are all suffering; let's let the past be buried too. But

Eric's mother only suffered more grief when they came to visit, and after a while they stopped coming.

At first Eric felt he had to accept it and he said nothing. But after a few months he told his mother, "I guess I can understand how *you* feel, but *I* want to visit Grandma and Grandpa and I think you should let me go by myself." At first his mother cried and yelled. She said mean things like, "Don't you care about what they did to me?" Eric kept quiet. A few days later his mother said, "I'm sorry, Eric, I shouldn't have said those things to you. If you want to visit your grandparents over the Easter vacation, I'll put you on the bus and they can meet you at the other end."

We need to realize just how important other grownups become when a parent dies, and then we need to find the people who can comfort us the most.

NEEDING OTHER PEOPLE: CHILDREN

Adults of all ages can be helpful, or not so helpful —age has nothing to do with it. That's not so with children—age may make a great deal of difference. Let me tell you about Margo and Edith. When their father died Margo was thirteen and Edith was nine.

Margo had always been a very studious girl—quiet, shy, always reading books and writing poetry. She had not had an easy time making friends. Edith, on the other hand, was always "the life of the party." She was very funny, she always had lots of good ideas for games to play; she had more friends than she knew what to do with.

After their father died, a very strange thing happened. Within a few months the situation had reversed itself completely. Margo had half a dozen new, good friends and Edith felt alone and deserted. There was a logical explanation for this change. Margo's age group was better able to understand Margo's feelings; they were not quite as frightened by what had happened to her. Margo said, "It was such a strange thing; girls who never used to notice me before seemed to want to let me know that they sympathized with me. They did such nice things! They began inviting me to their houses, they admired my clothes, they said they thought I wrote the best stories of anyone in the class. They were so thoughtful and they seemed so sincere that I stopped feeling so shy. I found out how much I liked having friends. It made me feel excited and happy. I found out that I could be a good friend to them, too. It changed my whole life. I guess most girls my age like to talk about their feelings."

Edith had some very painful experiences. Some of her best friends began to avoid her. They seemed

very embarrassed and uneasy when they saw her. Sometimes she would approach several children and realize that as soon as they saw her coming, they would look the other way or begin walking away from her. It seemed that she had not only lost her father but all of her friends as well.

There was a new boy in her class. He seemed friendly until one day he asked, "Where does your father work?" When Edith said, "My father is dead," the boy walked away from her without saying a word and never spoke to her again. Edith said, "I felt like I had some terrible disease and the other kids were afraid of catching it."

That is *exactly* what was happening. Most children Edith's age just don't know how to talk to someone whose parent has died. In addition, the very thought of a parent dying is so terrifying that they don't want to be near anyone who could remind them that once in a while such a terrible thing does happen.

One day Edith said something that made one of the boys in her class get angry at her. He said, "You think you're so smart, just because your father tells the news on television!" Edith replied, "My father died." The boy yelled, "Well, I hope your whole family dies!" Edith burst into tears and ran out of the room. She met the principal in the hall and he took her to his office. The principal told Edith that he could understand how she felt and he was very sorry this had happened, but that some children had things that bothered them and sometimes took it out on other people. He said, "Something must be hurting Ronny very much for him to be so mean to you."

Edith tried to understand but she really couldn't. It hurt and hurt. But she didn't tell her mother about it. Then something else happened. There was a girl in another class whose mother had been badly burned in a car accident. (She had died several weeks later.) One day Edith heard Ronny shouting at the other girl, "Ha, ha—your mother was bar-becued!" This time Edith told her mother both stories. Now she was *really* mad. Her mother agreed that such things could not be allowed to go on. Sometimes a grownup has to step in and help. She called the boy's mother and said she wanted to come over and see her. The boy's mother began to cry on the phone. Her husband had left her and she didn't even know where he was. She said she real-ized she and her son needed help and she was going to ask the pediatrician to recommend a place for them to go for counseling.

Edith's friends still stayed away from her, and, for a little while, Edith just gave up on her friends. She stayed by herself and she cried about feeling lonely. Then one day she decided she could try again. There was a girl in her class whose father had died when she was only sixteen months old. Edith began to talk to this girl one day about their going bicycling together after school. The girl was very friendly. They made a date and had a very good time. They became friends. Much later on, Darlene said, "You know, you are really luckier than I am. You know when your father's birthday is and you can remember being at his parties. I can't remember anything." Edith suddenly felt very sorry for Darlene. As they talked, Edith began to understand how hard it is to show sympathy to someone else, and she began to understand why some children had run away from her. Over the next few months, she began to make friends again.

LIFE BEGINS TO CHANGE

Slowly but surely, your life begins to get back to normal. But just about the time you begin to think everything is settling down, all kinds of *new* things may begin to happen which may shake you up all over again. Your mother may be offered a much better job in another city; your father may begin to bring one of his dates home more and more often and you realize he's thinking about getting married again. You feel scared of moving to a new neighborhood and a new school. You feel *very* scared of having a new mother. Suppose she turns out to be awful, or she doesn't love you? Sometimes, your mother or father falls in love with someone who has children of his or her own. What's going to happen then, with a whole bunch of stepsisters and stepbrothers living in *your* house?

One of the most important things to remember is that children cannot and should not have the responsibility of making any decisions about whom and when a parent remarries. Hopefully this will be a subject that a parent and children can discuss together, openly and honestly, but all final decisions must be made by the parent.

Melanie and her sister Jennifer were eight and ten years old when their mother began going out with men some months after their father died. After a while they realized that there were just two men that their mother seemed really to care about. One was a very rich man with a beautiful sailboat and a Mercedes Benz. He was very handsome and wore elegant clothes. Every time he came to the house he brought fancy presents for the girls. The other man was a schoolteacher. He seemed kind of bossy. He scolded the girls when they stayed up too late. Melanie and Jennifer thought it was none of his business. They were hoping their mother would marry the rich man. When she told them she was going to marry the teacher, they were very upset. They were sure he'd be very strict. Melanie said, "If you marry Greg, I want to go away to boarding school! I don't want to live with him!" Her mother said, "I'm sorry you feel that way, but I'm the mother and you're the child and you will just have to trust my judgment. I must marry the person I love. We will do everything we can to help you get used to it."

As things turned out, the girls discovered that the reason Greg was strict was because he really cared what happened to them. They liked him more and more—and it was great having a teacher to help them with their homework!

Becoming a new family, with a new parent and possibly new brothers and sisters, is very difficult even under the best of circumstances. Everybody feels self-conscious and uneasy. You have a feeling it just won't work out. How can a stranger become one of your parents?

First of all, the new parent is probably as scared as you are! He or she doesn't know exactly how to act. Nobody wants you to forget your biological parent, but on the other hand, if you make comparisons all the time, it will be impossible for you to move on to new relationships. Stepparents worry a great deal about being too strict or not strict enough. They want to be loved, and they want to love you, but many times these feelings don't get communicated. It is important to remember that the new parent may be just as mixed up and uncertain as you are.

Time is very, very important. It is helpful if no one becomes too impatient. Don't think that if the first few months are very stormy that means it is never going to get any better. After a while you will probably discover that just living together and having family experiences together begins slowly but surely to make you feel part of a new family group.

Sometimes you begin to like your new mother or father before he or she actually comes to live with you and the first weeks together seem absolutely perfect. Then, after a while, people are no longer on their best behavior. The new parent gets tired or cranky; you can't get used to his or her ideas about rules and you get mad and begin to fight back. People begin to say things in anger that they may not really mean. There are hurt feelings and long silences.

We need to remember that such things occur in *every* family. If both parents and children try hard to share their feelings and understand and respect one another, such problems will be solved in time.

Even a bad beginning can turn out all right later on. Ed was sent to a sleep-away camp two summers after his father had died. His mother had been going out with several men but she hadn't said anything about getting married. And she never said anything about it when she came to visit him. The day he came home from camp his mother informed him that she and Martin had gotten married and they would now be living with Martin's three children in a different house. Ed was speechless as his mother drove him home from the train station. He was furious. At first all he could think about was that all his possessions had been moved without his even knowing what was going on. But when he reached the house, the shock really hit him; when he opened that door there would be a new father he did not know very well and three brothers and sisters he had met only once before.

It is hard to imagine a worse beginning. This happened many years ago and most parents have learned to prepare their children more carefully for such big changes. But even in this situation, it worked out much better than Ed ever thought it could. As it turned out, it was fun having a big family—there was always someone to play with. Of course, there were fights and the children felt jealous of the attention their own parent was paying to his or her new children, but in later years they realized that in spite of that beginning, they had learned to care about each other.

Once in a while a parent makes a mistake. Sometimes the new marriage does not work out very well. It may even end in divorce. This is particularly painful after you have already suffered so much. In many such cases, both grownups and children may need to see someone special to help understand their feelings and problems.

GETTING SPECIAL HELP

I have mentioned several times that it might be important for you to get special help. It is time to explain what that means.

Six months after his mother's death Tony was having bad nightmares; he was also failing at school. When he was not in school he just seemed to want to sit in his room, not doing anything. His father tried to talk to him, but Tony just kept saying he wanted to be left alone. His father went to talk to his teacher and she suggested that Tony and his dad talk to someone at the Community Mental Health Clinic. This is a place where specially trained staff members help people who have problems deal with their feelings. There are usually three kinds of professionals at such places—social workers, psychologists, and psychiatrists. These are professions in which people get special training to understand the problems of children, grownups, and families.

Tony's father made the first appointment for himself. There he spoke to a social worker. He told the social worker what had been happening ever since Tony's mother had died.

Tony went along on the next visit. He met a

woman who was a psychologist. She took him into a very cheerful room with things like paint and clay to play with. They sat at a table and talked and the woman asked Tony some questions and they played a few interesting games together.

On the next visit, Tony's father talked to the social worker and Tony met a man who was a psychiatrist. The man said he and Tony would be talking together once a week for a while. At first Tony was very shy and careful. He didn't want to tell the psychiatrist anything about how he was feeling. But after a few weeks, he really began to like Dr. Lewis. He was very surprised at finding out how smart Dr. Lewis was about what he was feeling.

One day they were playing a game of checkers. For the first time Tony won. He got very excited and began jumping around the room. "I beat you! I beat you!" he was shouting. He felt kind of happy for the first time since his mother had gotten sick. And then all of a sudden he got terribly afraid. He ran over to Dr. Lewis, pushed all the checkers off the table, and said, "It's only a stupid game." Dr. Lewis said, "Tony, did you do that because you were afraid to beat me? Did you think *I* might get sick and die?" Tony was furious. What a dumb thing for the doctor to say. He stormed out of the office saying, "I'm never coming back here—you're stupid!" Dr. Lewis didn't get angry. He said, "I'm sorry you're so upset, Tony. I'll see you next week."

Because he really trusted Dr. Lewis, Tony came back. For the next few weeks they talked a lot about that checkers game. After a while Tony remembered an incident that he had completely forgotten. It happened the very day his mother got sick and had to go to the hospital. It was a rainy afternoon. When he'd gotten home from school his mother was in bed. She said she didn't feel well. But Tony was bored and didn't feel like playing alone and so he had kept nagging his mother to play with him. Finally she gave in, came into the dining room, and they started to play Monopoly.

Tony was very good at the game and he was buying many houses and hotels. Several times his mother said she didn't feel well and wanted to go back to bed, but Tony kept saying, "Just a little longer." Then, suddenly, his mother got a terrible pain in her chest. She told Tony to call his father. She lay on the floor in the dining room with her eyes closed until the doctor came and took her away in an ambulance.

On the day that Tony remembered this experience, he began to sob in Dr. Lewis's office. "I killed her! I killer her!" he cried. Dr. Lewis held Tony very tight. He talked to him very quietly. He said, "No you didn't, Tony. Your mother had a heart condition from the time she was a little girl.

Paul Giovanopoulos

She lived longer than anyone had expected her to —probably because she loved you and your dad so much. She loved playing with you. She was going to die very soon, anyway. Playing with you was something that made her happy. Even though she had to stay in bed often you had no way of knowing how ill she really was. But because you *thought* it was your fault, you felt so frightened and guilty that you forgot all about what happened on that day."

Tony went on seeing Dr. Lewis for several months. Tony had never been able to mourn for his mother in a natural way, but with Dr. Lewis's help he now began to have some confidence in himself.

The reason people sometimes need special help with their feelings is because of the way our minds work. You may know that everyone has conscious feelings and unconscious feelings. When we are dreaming, our unconscious mind is at work. When we forget something, it doesn't just disappear; it stays in the unconscious part of our minds. Because of our unconscious feelings, we sometimes get mixed-up ideas. Tony's thinking he killed his mother is one of those confused ideas. It was such a painful idea that he "forgot" it, but it stayed on in his unconscious mind. The reason he felt so afraid and couldn't concentrate in school was because those "forgotten" thoughts were really bothering him a lot.

It is natural to be sad and unhappy for a long time when a parent dies. But sometimes these feelings go on for such a long time that you just can't bear it any longer. And sometimes these feelings seem to affect everything you do. If that happens, then it is probably time to talk to your mother or father or someone at school or your doctor or minister about getting special help.

A social worker, psychologist, or psychiatrist is specially trained to help us find out more about our other unconscious feelings. When we find out what those feelings are and can think about them consciously, we can begin to clear them up. We can figure out what makes sense and what doesn't make sense.

There are many people who can help you when you feel troubled. Sometimes, just talking to your doctor or your minister, priest or rabbi may help. These days people in many professions have special training in helping people with their troubled feelings. When the unhappiness seems very strong and goes on for a long time, you and your mother or father may need to see someone for a longer period of time, as Tony did. Most communities now have some kind of mental-health services. If you live in a big city there is usually a council of social agencies or a branch of the Family Services Association which can help you and your mother or father find the right place to go. If you live in a small town or in a rural area, there may be a college or a university where you can get such information. Often the best place to start to find out is through the school nurse or guidance counselor. There is one clinic in the United States that specializes in helping children with their feelings when a parent dies: the Situational Crisis Service, The Center for Preventive Psychiatry, 340 Mamaroneck Ave., White Plains, N.Y., 10605.

Getting help with one's feelings is nothing to be ashamed of. Everyone goes through troubled times, and the death of a parent is so painful that many people just cannot recover from the blow without some professional help. Actually it takes a great deal of courage to admit that one needs help. It is a very wise and grown-up thing to do. After all, if you broke a leg you wouldn't try to fix it yourself; you know that you need someone who is trained to take care of such things. And we are lucky to live in a time when there are people who know how to take care of those other kinds of wounds, too.

DEATH TEACHES US ABOUT LIFE

꿏꘏(|)꘍꿏

If any of you have ever visited some of the oldest graveyards in this country—mostly around New England—you have probably seen the grave markers which tell how many children died, how many mothers died in childbirth, how many parents and children died from diseases that you have never even heard about.

Years ago, most people died at home in their beds. Up until the last century or so, few people went to hospitals and there were no funeral chapels. Death was such a common part of everyday life that children shared in whatever experiences their families might go through with dying relatives. Families still loved each other very much and grieved over these deaths, but they were not so un-expected. Death was a familiar and inevitable part of life.

The scientific discoveries of the last 100 years have changed all that. Many diseases have been conquered; operations are far safer; childbirth is safer, and serious diseases among very young children are far less common. We also have better nutrition, better dental care and other kinds of preventive medical care. Our lives are longer and healthier.

Gradually, death became more removed from daily life. Few people died at home. Mostly it was old people who died. Children and parents could live for long periods of time without ever hearing about the death of someone they loved. Unhappily, no generation has ever lived without hearing about people dying in wars, and there have been terrible wars in the last few generations. But in spite of this, the fact of death was seen and talked about less and less. It was almost as if people thought that if no one talked about death, maybe it would just go away!

During this period, parents were inclined to protect their children—they did not take them to funerals, they tried not to cry or show their grief in front of their children, and they did not talk to them about dying.

Recently, people have begun to realize that such

attitudes were very foolish. When a death occurred, neither grownups nor children had any idea what to do or even how to feel. And since death had been treated as something too ugly and terrible ever to mention, people who were dying were often very lonely. Nobody would let them talk about their fears; nobody would ever say an honest good-by. And many children grew up feeling very embarrassed about death, not knowing how to act or what to say. They wondered about death but were afraid to ask any questions.

Fortunately, all that is changing now. All over the country there are people studying and working and writing about this problem. Part of the work is to help people who know they are dying to express their feelings, to feel close to the people they love, and to have an opportunity to say their good-bys— to die with dignity, still feeling that they are part of their families. And we are finding ways to help relatives and friends stay close to someone who is dying. We have also learned that children suffer very much when they are shut out, when they do not get the help they need to face the death of someone they love.

We cannot really hide from death; it is a part of life. But when we begin to face the meaning of death, we can learn a great deal about how to live and the meaning of life.

A famous playwright, George Bernard Shaw,

said, "Heartbreak is life educating us." Can you figure out what that means? I think it means that when something happens which makes us feel very sad, we learn something new and important about how wonderful it is to be alive. The heartbreak of having a parent die teaches us just how valuable a human being can be—just how precious and special. Such an experience teaches us that life is sacred.

Your mother or father was different from anyone else in all the world. There never was anyone just like him or her—and there never will be. What a remarkable idea that is! If we were all the same, it wouldn't matter so much when one person died. The loss of someone is so painful because of that uniqueness. We can find other people to love, but each love is special and different.

Another lesson that death teaches us is that nobody ever dies completely. When someone dies we discover how much he or she left behind. It seems unbelievable when you begin to think about it. Each person who lives changes the world in some small or big way and leaves much of him or herself to those who live afterward. Children, of course, are a beautiful gift for a parent to leave the world. Or a teacher may leave behind hundreds of children who will remember that he or she could teach arithmetic so that every single child had fun and didn't ever feel dumb. Or a house painter may leave behind a lot of happy families living in pretty houses. Or a good cook leaves behind lots of wonderful recipes for people to enjoy for generations. Or a mother teaches her baby special lullabies that her mother taught her and that her children will teach their children. Or maybe a fireman saves the life of a child who becomes a doctor and saves other people's lives.

A person leaves behind many memories and many deeds. Even if you were very young when he or she died, you have been influenced more than you may realize. You can never lose a person completely; he or she will be a part of you all your life. I know a man whose father died when he was very young. The man could not remember much about his father at all. When he became a father himself, Larry discovered that he could "make up" wonderful stories that his little daughter Wendy wanted to hear over and over again. When her friends came to visit they would whisper to her, "Tell your father to tell us the story of Trunky again."

So many children loved Larry's stories that a few years later some of them were published so more children could enjoy them. An aunt of Larry's saw one of these little storybooks and said, "Do you know that this is almost exactly the story your father used to tell you when you were about three or four years old? He was wonderful at making up stories." Larry's father had left him a gift without Larry's even realizing it.

Most of you are old enough to have many memories. But some of these may fade with time. You probably want to remember as much as you can. Perhaps you'd like to make a special scrapbook, not just of pictures, but stories that you want to write down or things that happened that you want to remember. A scrapbook might include all kinds of memories—the boat trip on the Mississippi when you were all so happy together; the time you got so scared when Dad got a speeding ticket because he was driving too fast; the day when you were on vacation and your mother taught you how to make tollhouse cookies; the time she threw a shoe at you because she was so mad at the mess in your room.

Someday you might want to tell your own child about your mother or father. Recording your ideas and memories now would not only give you a permanent record, but it would also help you to realize just how rich you are in all the things you have received from your parent. One girl who decided to write down all the things she could think of about her father said, "My daddy was a writer, and I think I'll be one too. This will be my first book. I think I inherited this talent from him." A boy who was eight years old when his father died got very excited when he was about eleven. His arms began to get hairy. He told his mother, "Look, Mom, I'm getting reddish hair on my hands and arms—just like Daddy's!"

SAYING GOOD-BY

At the same time that memories are good to have, life goes on and we need to think about the present and the future. It takes most families about a year before they are ready to say a real good-by to the person who has died.

This is the story of how that happened in one family. You may have noticed that this book is dedicated to Bob Kennedy and to his two daughters, Suzanne and Elizabeth. Bob and his wife Beverly had been my friends for about ten years before Bob died. My husband and I first met Liz and Suzie when they were about two and four years old. We have loved them very, very much. After Bob died, Bev and the two girls (then eight and ten) came to visit us. When they walked in the door I said to them, "The worst thing that could happen to you has now happened." We cried and cried and held each other very tight. That was how this book began. I wanted to write down all the things that we shared in our grief. I thought that what Liz and Suzie taught me might be helpful to other children.

It was about a year after Bob Kennedy died that I finished writing this book. At about the same time, my husband and I were with Bob's wife and two daughters for a summer vacation. Suzie and Liz still cried at times, and we talked a lot about their dad. They talked about good times and bad times. They both told me, "Daddy wasn't perfect," and their love for him included his weaknesses and his strengths. We laughed a lot, too. We talked about all the different kinds of feelings they have had ever since their father died. The sadness will never leave them completely, but their father's death is not going to keep them from having rich and happy lives.

My husband and I, Bev, and the two girls went to the cemetery together. We bought two flowering bushes and planted them near the headstone. It was raining very hard, and we all huddled together under one umbrella, crying and hugging each other. I read a letter I'd written to Bob—not really for him but for us:

Dear Bob:

We are here together—your family—to celebrate your life. It is almost a year since you died, and yet you are still with us in so many ways. We think about you and talk about you so much. We have spent this past week on Cape Cod and everywhere we went we remembered being there with you. It would be foolish to pretend we have not been sad. You were such a special person, so full of life and joy that you made everyone else around you feel a sharper awareness of the pleasures in being alive.

No one was ever like you and nobody ever will be like you—and we miss you terribly. But there is another kind of feeling too, and that is how lucky we all were to have had you in our lives.

Bev and Liz and Suzie have gone on living their lives just as you would have wanted them to do. In spite of missing you we laugh and we joke. We learn new things. We make new friends. We fight with each other and then we make up. Every day we find new wonders and pleasures and we try to live our lives as fully as you did. We know that what you would want more than anything else is for us to remember you by living and loving.

Bev has been working very hard. Liz has made some wonderful new friends and goes ice-skating almost every day. Suzie tells stories and jokes just the way you used to do. She is now the family comedian, as you once were. Both of your daughters learned the most important messages you wanted them to learn—to trust other people, to be curious, to reach out to others with interest and compassion. I wish you could see the way they "interview" people on beaches and buses and boats—just the way you did on your television program!

We are not afraid to talk about you and to remember—good times and bad times, happy times and sad times. We are not afraid to feel our feelings.

We remember being with you in so many places, having so much fun. We talk about you with all the people who knew you. All the good and kind things you did for all of us keep you alive in the world. We stand here with our arms around each other knowing that in this moment of loving, you are here with us.

When I finished reading this letter, Liz looked very thoughtful. I could tell she was trying to think of some special message she would like to give to her father. Suddenly she ran and did a cartwheel on her daddy's grave. Her mother whispered to me, "Liz hasn't done any cartwheels since Bob died. He used to love it when she did."

I tried to understand just what Liz's message to her father meant. Then I realized that her gift to

him was to pick up the threads of her life and to begin to live as fully as she could. The time comes to begin to do cartwheels again—to express our joy in being alive. That is the very best kind of good-by to a parent who has died.

FURTHER
READING

❧❦❧

FOR CHILDREN

NONFICTION

Klein, Stanley. *The Final Mystery*. New York: Doubleday, 1974.

LeShan, Eda. *What Makes Me Feel This Way?* Chapter 10, "The Fear of Death and Dying." New York: Macmillan, 1972.

Zim, Herbert, *Life and Death*. New York: Morrow, 1970.

FICTION

(For children under eight years of age)

DePaola, Tomie. *Nana Upstairs and Nana Downstairs*. New York: Putnam, 1973.

Dobrin, Arnold. *Scat*. New York: Four Winds Press, 1971.

Fassler, Joan. *My Grandpa Died Today*. New York: Behavioral Publications, 1971.

Kantrowitz, Mildred. *When Violet Died*. New York: Parents Magazine Press, 1973.

Miles, Miska. *Annie and the Old One*. Boston: Little, Brown, 1971.

Shector, Ben. *Across the Meadow*. New York: Doubleday, 1973.

(For ages eight to twelve)

Carlson, Natalie. *The Half Sisters*. New York: Harper & Row, 1970.

Cleaver, Vera and Bill. *Grover*. Philadelphia: Lippincott, 1970.

Orgel, Doris. *The Mulberry Music*. New York: Harper & Row, 1970.

Shector, Ben. *Someplace Else.* New York: Harper & Row, 1971.

Smith, Doris Buchanan. *A Taste of Blackberries.* New York: T. Y. Crowell, 1973.

Tresselt, Alvin. *The Dead Tree.* New York: Parents Magazine Press, 1972.

(For ages eleven to fourteen)

Degens, T. *Transport 7—41—R.* New York: Viking, 1974.

Donovan, John. *I'll Get There. It Better Be Worth the Trip.* New York: Harper & Row, 1971.

Fenton, Edward. *A Matter of Miracles.* New York: Holt, Rinehart & Winston, 1967.

Hunter, Mollie. *A Sound of Chariots.* New York: Harper & Row, 1972.

Mohr, Nicholasa. *Nilda.* New York: Harper & Row, 1973.

Rosenthal, Ted. *How Could I Not Be Among You?* New York: Braziller, 1973.

FOR PARENTS

Furman, Erna. *A Child's Parent Dies.* New Haven, Conn.: Yale University Press, 1974.

Grollman, Earl A. *Talking About Death*. Boston: Beacon Press, 1970.

Grollman, Earl A., ed. *Explaining Death to Children*. Boston: Beacon Press, 1967.

Jackson, Edgar. *Telling a Child About Death*. Channel Press, 1965.

————. *You and Your Grief*. Channel Press, 1961.

————. *Understanding Grief*. New York: Abingdon Press, 1951.

Kliman, Gilbert, M.D. *Psychological Emergencies of Childhood*. New York: Grune & Stratton, 1968.